Risks and Vulnerabilities of the US Economy Due to Overspending and Printing Dollars

Copyright Page

TITLE: Risks and Vulnerabilities of the US Economy Due to Overspending and Printing Dollars

1ST Edition

Table of Contents

Risks and Vulnerabilities of the US Economy Due to Overspending and Printing Dollars

By Roberto Miguel Rodriguez

Book Organization

The Impact of Overspending and Increased Money Supply on Inflation Rates

- Introduction to the concept of inflation and its relationship with overspending and increased money supply.

- Case studies highlighting historical instances of inflation and its detrimental effects.

- Analysis of the current US economic landscape and the potential risks of inflation due to overspending.

- Examination of the role of the Federal Reserve in managing inflation and its effectiveness.

The Role of Foreign Debt in Exacerbating the US Deficit Crisis

- Explanation of the US deficit crisis and its connection to foreign debt.

- Analysis of the impact of foreign debt on the US economy and its potential vulnerabilities.

- Examination of the consequences of relying on foreign countries for financing the deficit.

- Case studies illustrating the potential risks and vulnerabilities associated with foreign debt.

The Long-Term Consequences of Printing More American Dollars on the Value of the Currency

- Exploration of the relationship between the value of the US dollar and continuous printing of money.

- Analysis of the potential risks and vulnerabilities associated with devaluing the currency.

- Examination of the impact on international trade and the US's position as a global economic power.

- Case studies highlighting the long-term consequences faced by countries that have devalued their currencies.

The Connection Between Overspending and Income Inequality in the US

- Examination of the correlation between overspending, income inequality, and wealth distribution.

- Analysis of the economic implications of income inequality on the overall US economy.

- Discussion on potential policy measures to address income inequality and its relationship with overspending.

- Case studies showcasing the impact of income inequality on various sectors of the economy.

The Economic Implications of Overspending and Increased Money Supply on Small Businesses

- Analysis of the challenges faced by small businesses due to overspending and increased money supply.

- Examination of the impact on entrepreneurship, job creation, and economic growth.

- Case studies illustrating the struggles and vulnerabilities of small businesses in an overspending economy.

- Discussion on potential solutions and support mechanisms for small businesses.

The Effect of the US Deficit on Interest Rates and Borrowing Costs

- Explanation of the relationship between the US deficit, interest rates, and borrowing costs.

- Analysis of the potential risks and vulnerabilities associated with high interest rates and borrowing costs.

- Examination of the impact on consumer spending, investments, and economic stability.

- Case studies showcasing the consequences of high interest rates and borrowing costs in different economic scenarios.

The Relationship Between Overspending and the National Debt, and Its Impact on Future Generations

- Exploration of the connection between overspending, national debt, and intergenerational equity.

- Analysis of the long-term consequences faced by future generations due to excessive debt.

- Discussion on potential strategies to reduce the national debt and protect the interests of future generations.

- Case studies highlighting the burden of national debt on different countries and their future prospects.

The Influence of Overspending on Global Financial Markets and International Trade

- Examination of the impact of US overspending on global financial markets and international trade.

- Analysis of the vulnerabilities and risks faced by global economies due to US overspending.

- Discussion on potential measures to mitigate the negative effects on international trade and financial stability.

- Case studies illustrating the influence of US overspending on global economic dynamics.

The Political Implications of Overspending and Increased Money Supply on Government Policies and Decision-Making

- Exploration of the political landscape surrounding overspending and increased money supply.

- Analysis of the influence of economic factors on government policies and decision-making processes.

- Discussion on potential reforms to improve fiscal responsibility and accountability.

- Case studies showcasing the political implications of overspending in different countries and their governance.

The Potential Risks and Vulnerabilities of the US Economy Due to Continuous Overspending and Printing More American Dollars

- Summary of the main risks and vulnerabilities discussed throughout the book.

- Analysis of the potential consequences of failing to address overspending and increased money supply.

- Discussion on the importance of public awareness and economic literacy in shaping a sustainable future.

- Conclusion and recommendations for policymakers, economists, and the general public.

This book aims to provide a comprehensive analysis of the potential risks and vulnerabilities of the US economy due to continuous overspending and printing more American dollars. By delving into specific aspects such as inflation rates, foreign debt, currency devaluation, income inequality, small businesses, interest rates, national debt, global financial markets, political implications, and future generations, this book offers valuable insights for economists and the public alike. The thorough examination of research findings, case studies, and detailed analysis aims to empower readers with a deeper understanding of the economic implications of overspending and increased money supply.

Chapter 1: The Impact of Overspending and Increased Money Supply on Inflation Rates

The Relationship Between Government Spending and Inflation

In today's economic landscape, the relationship between government spending and inflation has become a critical concern for economists and the public alike. This subchapter aims to shed light on the various facets of this complex relationship, examining its impact on inflation rates, the role of foreign debt, long-term consequences on the currency's value, connection to income inequality, implications for small businesses, effect on interest rates and borrowing costs, impact on future generations, influence on global financial markets and international trade, political implications, as well as the potential risks and vulnerabilities it poses to the US economy.

One of the key concerns surrounding government spending and increased money supply is its impact on inflation rates. As the government injects more money into the economy through spending, it can lead to an excess supply of money, which often results in rising prices. This can erode the purchasing power of individuals and businesses, leading to inflationary pressures.

Moreover, the role of foreign debt exacerbates the US deficit crisis, as the government becomes increasingly reliant on borrowing from foreign entities to fund its spending. This not only increases the overall national debt but also poses risks to the country's economic stability and sovereignty.

The long-term consequences of printing more American dollars are also worrisome. Excessive money printing can lead to a devaluation of the currency, as more dollars flood the market. This can have far-reaching implications for international trade and can undermine the US dollar's status as the global reserve currency.

Furthermore, overspending has been linked to income inequality in the US. As the government allocates more resources towards certain sectors or programs, it can exacerbate disparities in income distribution, widening the gap between the rich and the poor.

The economic implications of overspending and increased money supply on small businesses should not be underestimated. Small businesses often struggle to adapt to rising costs and inflation, potentially leading to closures and job losses.

The US deficit also has a direct impact on interest rates and borrowing costs. As the government borrows more to finance its spending, it competes with private borrowers for funds, driving up interest rates and making borrowing more expensive for businesses and individuals.

Moreover, overspending and the resulting national debt have significant implications for future generations. As the debt continues to accumulate, future generations will inherit the burden of repaying it, potentially limiting their economic opportunities and well-being.

The influence of overspending extends beyond domestic borders, affecting global financial markets and international trade. The US economy's size and interconnectedness mean that any disruptions caused by excessive spending can have ripple effects worldwide.

The political implications of overspending and increased money supply cannot be ignored. Government policies and decision-making are often influenced by the need to finance spending, potentially leading to short-term fixes rather than long-term sustainable solutions.

Finally, continuous overspending and printing more American dollars expose the US economy to a range of risks and vulnerabilities. These include a loss of investor confidence, a weakened financial system, and an increased susceptibility to economic shocks.

In conclusion, the relationship between government spending and inflation is a multifaceted issue with wide-ranging implications. Understanding the impact of overspending and increased money supply on inflation rates, foreign debt, currency value, income inequality, small businesses, interest rates, future generations, global markets, and political decision-making is crucial to safeguarding the US economy from potential risks and vulnerabilities. It is imperative that economists and the public remain vigilant and informed about the consequences of continuous overspending and printing more American dollars.

The Effect of Increased Money Supply on Price Levels

In the ongoing debate surrounding the US economy, one crucial aspect that demands attention is the effect of increased money supply on price levels. The continuous overspending and printing of more American dollars have significant implications for economists and the public alike.

One immediate impact of overspending and increased money supply is the inflation rates. As the government pumps more money into the economy, the purchasing power of each dollar decreases. This, in turn, leads to a rise in the overall price levels of goods and services. Economists have long established a positive correlation between money supply and inflation, highlighting the detrimental consequences of excessive monetary expansion.

Furthermore, the role of foreign debt cannot be ignored in exacerbating the US deficit crisis. As the government continues to borrow from foreign countries to finance its overspending, the national debt surges to unprecedented levels. This not only burdens future generations with mounting interest payments but also weakens the overall economic stability of the nation.

The long-term consequences of printing more American dollars also have implications for the value of the currency. As the money supply expands, the value of the dollar depreciates, making imports more expensive and reducing the purchasing power of US consumers. This can lead to a decline in economic competitiveness and potentially harm the balance of trade.

Moreover, overspending and increased money supply have been linked to income inequality in the US. As the government focuses on financing its spendings, it often neglects investments in education, infrastructure, and social welfare programs. This exacerbates the gap between the rich and the poor, leading to social unrest and economic instability.

Small businesses also face the brunt of overspending and increased money supply. As inflation rises, the cost of production and raw materials increases, making it harder for small businesses to compete. This can stifle entrepreneurship and hinder economic growth.

The US deficit also has a direct impact on interest rates and borrowing costs. As the government borrows more, the demand for credit increases, leading to higher interest rates. This can discourage investment and hinder economic expansion.

Furthermore, overspending and the national debt have long-term implications for future generations. The burden of financing the debt falls on the shoulders of the young, who will inherit an economy burdened with interest payments and limited fiscal flexibility.

The influence of overspending extends beyond national borders, affecting global financial markets and international trade. As the US continues to rely on borrowed funds, it becomes increasingly vulnerable to fluctuations in global markets, potentially leading to financial crises with global ramifications.

Lastly, the political implications of overspending and increased money supply cannot be ignored. The government's policies and decision-making are heavily influenced by the need to finance its spendings, often leading to short-term fixes rather than long-term sustainable solutions.

In conclusion, the potential risks and vulnerabilities of the US economy due to continuous overspending and printing more American dollars are vast. From inflation and income inequality to global market volatility and political implications, the consequences of increased money supply on price levels are far-reaching. It is imperative for economists and the public to understand and address these issues to ensure a stable and prosperous future for the nation.

The Role of Monetary Policy in Controlling Inflation

Inflation is a persistent concern for any economy, and the role of monetary policy in controlling it is of utmost importance. This subchapter explores the various aspects of how monetary policy impacts inflation rates and its wider implications on the US economy.

One of the key topics discussed is the impact of overspending and increased money supply on inflation rates. As the government spends more and prints more American dollars, the excess money in circulation leads to an increase in demand, which ultimately drives up prices. Economists and the public need to understand the intricate link between overspending and inflation and its consequences for the overall economy.

Another crucial aspect highlighted is the role of foreign debt in exacerbating the US deficit crisis. The US heavily relies on borrowing from foreign nations to finance its spending, resulting in a growing deficit. This subchapter delves into the implications of this debt on inflation rates and the challenges it poses for the US economy as a whole.

Furthermore, it explores the long-term consequences of continuously printing more American dollars on the value of the currency. The excessive printing of money can erode the value of the dollar, leading to a loss of purchasing power for individuals and businesses. This, in turn, affects the economy's competitiveness and can have adverse effects on the global financial markets and international trade.

The subchapter also sheds light on the connection between overspending and income inequality in the US. As the government redirects resources towards its spending priorities, it can exacerbate income disparities, leading to a more unequal society. This has implications not only for social stability but also for economic growth and long-term sustainability.

Additionally, the economic implications of overspending and increased money supply on small businesses are examined. Small businesses often face the brunt of inflation, as they may struggle to absorb rising costs or pass them onto consumers. This subchapter highlights the challenges faced by small businesses and the potential impact on job creation and economic growth.

The effect of the US deficit on interest rates and borrowing costs is another important area of discussion. Overspending and increased debt levels can lead to higher interest rates and borrowing costs, affecting both businesses and individuals. Understanding this relationship is vital for economists and the public to grasp the broader implications of the deficit crisis.

Moreover, the subchapter delves into the relationship between overspending, the national debt, and its impact on future generations. The continuous accumulation of debt and overspending can burden future generations with the responsibility of repayment, limiting their opportunities and economic well-being.

The influence of overspending on global financial markets and international trade is also explored. Excessive spending and increased money supply can create uncertainties and volatility in global markets, affecting investor confidence and trade relationships. Understanding these implications is crucial for economists and policymakers to make informed decisions regarding international economic relations.

Lastly, the subchapter addresses the political implications of overspending and increased money supply on government policies and decision-making. Overspending can be driven by political considerations, with governments prioritizing short-term gains over long-term stability. It is essential for economists and the public to understand the political dynamics that contribute to continuous overspending and its potential risks to the economy.

Overall, this subchapter aims to provide economists and the public with a comprehensive understanding of the role of monetary policy in controlling inflation and the potential risks and vulnerabilities of the US economy due to continuous overspending and printing more American dollars. By exploring various aspects, it equips readers with the knowledge to critically analyze and assess the current economic situation and contribute to informed discussions and decision-making processes.

The Historical Examples of Inflation Caused by Overspending

In the annals of economic history, there are several notable examples of inflation caused by overspending. These instances serve as cautionary tales, shedding light on the potential risks and vulnerabilities of continuous overspending and the printing of more American dollars. By examining these historical precedents, economists and the public can gain a deeper understanding of the impact of overspending and increased money supply on inflation rates.

One such historical example is the hyperinflation that plagued Germany in the 1920s. Following World War I, the German government resorted to excessive borrowing and printing money to finance its war reparations and social programs. This led to a rapid devaluation of the German mark, resulting in astronomical price increases. People needed wheelbarrows full of money just to buy basic necessities, and the value of the currency became virtually worthless. The devastating consequences of this hyperinflationary period serve as a stark reminder of the long-term consequences of printing more American dollars on the value of the currency.

Another example is the inflationary spiral experienced by Latin American countries in the 1980s and 1990s. Countries like Argentina and Brazil accumulated significant amounts of foreign debt, exacerbating their deficit crisis. To finance these debts, governments resorted to borrowing and printing money, leading to high inflation rates. Inflation eroded the purchasing power of the population, widening income inequality and exacerbating social unrest. This highlights the connection between overspending and income inequality in the US, as continuous overspending and increased money supply can disproportionately impact marginalized communities.

The economic implications of overspending and increased money supply on small businesses cannot be ignored either. Inflation erodes the profitability of small businesses, as they face rising costs of inputs and reduced consumer purchasing power. This can lead to business closures and job losses, further exacerbating economic inequality.

Moreover, overspending and the resulting deficit can have a significant impact on interest rates and borrowing costs. When the government borrows excessively, it competes with private borrowers for funds, driving up interest rates. Higher interest rates make borrowing more expensive for businesses and individuals, stifling investment and economic growth.

Furthermore, continuous overspending and the resulting national debt have severe consequences for future generations. As the debt burden grows, future generations will be burdened with higher taxes and reduced government spending on essential services like education and infrastructure.

The influence of overspending on global financial markets and international trade cannot be underestimated either. Excessive borrowing and money printing can lead to a loss of confidence in the US dollar, causing it to depreciate against other currencies. This can disrupt global financial stability and impact international trade, as the value of the US dollar plays a pivotal role in global transactions.

Lastly, overspending and increased money supply have significant political implications. Governments often resort to overspending and printing more money to finance popular programs and win favor with voters. However, these short-term gains can lead to long-term economic instability, affecting government policies and decision-making.

In conclusion, the historical examples of inflation caused by overspending provide valuable insights into the potential risks and vulnerabilities of the US economy due to continuous overspending and printing more American dollars. The impact on inflation rates, the role of foreign debt in exacerbating the deficit crisis, the long-term consequences on the currency's value, the connection to income inequality, the implications for small businesses, interest rates, and borrowing costs, the burden on future generations, the influence on global financial markets and international trade, and the political implications all serve as important lessons to be learned. It is crucial for economists and the public to understand these examples to make informed decisions and advocate for responsible fiscal policies.

Chapter 2: The Role of Foreign Debt in Exacerbating the US Deficit Crisis

The Growing Dependence on Foreign Borrowing

In recent years, the United States economy has witnessed a concerning trend: a growing dependence on foreign borrowing. This subchapter aims to shed light on the potential risks and vulnerabilities that arise as a result of this reliance, addressing economists and the public.

One of the immediate consequences of overspending and increased money supply is the impact on inflation rates. The influx of dollars into the economy can lead to a decrease in the value of the currency, resulting in higher prices for goods and services. This, in turn, affects the purchasing power of individuals and can create economic instability.

Furthermore, foreign debt plays a significant role in exacerbating the US deficit crisis. As the government borrows from foreign entities to finance its overspending, the national debt accumulates, putting a strain on future generations. The long-term consequences of printing more American dollars, such as reduced value of the currency, are exacerbated by this foreign borrowing, further increasing the vulnerability of the US economy.

The connection between overspending and income inequality in the US cannot be overlooked. As the government spends more and borrows to finance its expenditures, the burden of repayment falls on the taxpayers, widening the wealth gap. Small businesses also suffer as overspending and increased money supply lead to higher interest rates and borrowing costs, making it harder for them to thrive and compete.

The influence of overspending and increased money supply extends beyond domestic borders. The US deficit has a direct impact on interest rates and borrowing costs, affecting global financial markets and international trade. Moreover, the political implications of overspending and increased money supply cannot be ignored, as they shape government policies and decision-making.

Ultimately, the potential risks and vulnerabilities of the US economy due to continuous overspending and printing more American dollars are significant. It is essential for economists and the public to understand the consequences of this growing dependence on foreign borrowing. Only through awareness and informed decision-making can steps be taken to mitigate these risks and ensure a more stable and sustainable economic future for the United States.

The Effect of Foreign Debt on the US Economy

Foreign debt has had a significant impact on the US economy, with both short-term and long-term consequences. This subchapter explores the various ways in which foreign debt has affected the economy, highlighting its role in exacerbating the US deficit crisis and its implications on inflation rates, the value of the currency, income inequality, small businesses, interest rates, borrowing costs, future generations, global financial markets, international trade, and government policies.

One of the key connections between foreign debt and the US deficit crisis is the increased borrowing costs and interest rates. As the US borrows more money from foreign countries to finance its deficit, it becomes more dependent on external financing, leading to higher interest rates and borrowing costs. This not only affects the government's ability to fund its spending programs but also puts a burden on small businesses and individuals seeking loans.

Moreover, the overspending and increased money supply resulting from foreign debt have a direct impact on inflation rates. When the government prints more American dollars to finance its deficit, it leads to an increase in the money supply, which in turn can cause inflation. This has implications for the purchasing power of individuals and businesses, potentially leading to a decrease in the value of the currency.

Furthermore, the connection between overspending and income inequality cannot be ignored. As the government spends more and prints more money, it often benefits the wealthy and increases income inequality. The economic implications of overspending and increased money supply also extend to small businesses, which may struggle to compete in an inflationary environment and face increased borrowing costs.

In addition to these economic implications, foreign debt also has political implications. It influences government policies and decision-making, as the need to service the debt and maintain foreign investors' confidence becomes a priority. This can result in a restriction of policy options and limit the government's ability to address other pressing issues.

Finally, the long-term consequences of continuous overspending and printing more American dollars are significant. It not only burdens future generations with a massive national debt but also presents risks and vulnerabilities to the US economy. Excessive reliance on foreign debt can make the economy susceptible to external shocks and fluctuations in global financial markets and international trade.

In conclusion, foreign debt plays a crucial role in shaping the US economy and has far-reaching implications. From exacerbating the deficit crisis to impacting inflation rates, income inequality, small businesses, interest rates, borrowing costs, future generations, global financial markets, international trade, and government policies, the effect of foreign debt on the US economy cannot be ignored. It is imperative for policymakers, economists, and the public to understand these implications and work towards finding sustainable solutions to address the risks and vulnerabilities arising from continuous overspending and printing more American dollars.

The Risks and Vulnerabilities of Relying on Foreign Creditors

In the globalized world we live in today, the United States has become increasingly reliant on foreign creditors to finance its deficits. This subchapter explores the potential risks and vulnerabilities that arise from this dependence, shedding light on the profound consequences for the US economy and its citizens.

One of the key impacts of overspending and increased money supply on inflation rates is the erosion of purchasing power. When the government prints more American dollars to cover its deficits, it floods the market with excess currency, leading to a depreciation in its value. As a result, the cost of imports increases, pushing up prices for everyday goods and services, and ultimately reducing the standard of living for ordinary Americans.

Foreign debt exacerbates the US deficit crisis by adding an additional burden to an already unsustainable fiscal situation. As the US borrows from foreign countries to finance its spending, it accumulates a mounting debt that must be serviced through interest payments. This perpetuates a vicious cycle of borrowing to repay existing debts, creating a dangerous spiral that places a strain on the overall economy.

The long-term consequences of printing more American dollars on the value of the currency cannot be overlooked. As the supply of dollars increases, its value weakens, making it less attractive to foreign investors and diminishing its status as a global reserve currency. This loss of confidence in the US dollar can have severe implications for international trade and financial stability, potentially leading to a global economic downturn.

Overspending also plays a role in exacerbating income inequality in the US. As the government channels funds towards its own priorities, such as defense spending or entitlement programs, it neglects investments in education, healthcare, and infrastructure that could benefit the broader population. This growing wealth gap further erodes social cohesion and creates economic disparities that hinder long-term growth.

Furthermore, overspending and increased money supply have adverse effects on small businesses. These enterprises, which are the backbone of the US economy, often struggle to access affordable credit due to higher interest rates caused by the deficit. This restricts their growth potential, stifles innovation, and hampers job creation, all of which are crucial for a thriving economy.

The US deficit also directly impacts interest rates and borrowing costs. As the government competes for funds in the global market, it drives up interest rates, making it more expensive for businesses and individuals to borrow money. This restricts investment, dampens economic activity, and reduces overall competitiveness.

The national debt resulting from overspending and increased money supply has far-reaching implications for future generations. As the debt continues to accumulate, it places an enormous burden on future taxpayers who will be responsible for servicing and eventually repaying it. This hampers their ability to invest in their own future, stifles economic mobility, and undermines the intergenerational equity that is vital for a thriving society.

Overspending also has a profound influence on global financial markets and international trade. As the US government continues to borrow from foreign creditors, it becomes vulnerable to their economic and political interests. This dependence can compromise national security and limit the country's ability to act independently on the global stage.

Moreover, overspending and increased money supply have significant political implications. Governments are often incentivized to prioritize short-term electoral gains over long-term economic stability. The ability to spend more and print money can be politically advantageous, as it allows policymakers to fund popular programs without raising taxes. However, this short-sighted approach can lead to severe economic consequences, compromising the overall well-being of the nation.

In conclusion, the risks and vulnerabilities of relying on foreign creditors are manifold and have profound implications for the US economy. The impact of overspending and increased money supply on inflation rates, the role of foreign debt in exacerbating the US deficit crisis, and the long-term consequences of printing more American dollars on the value of the currency all highlight the urgent need for responsible fiscal management. Additionally, the connection between overspending and income inequality, the economic implications for small businesses, and the influence on interest rates and borrowing costs emphasize the wide-ranging effects of excessive spending. Finally, the national debt's impact on future generations, its influence on global financial markets and international trade, and its political implications underscore the gravity of the situation. It is imperative for economists and the public to understand these risks and vulnerabilities in order to advocate for sound fiscal policies that promote sustainable economic growth and safeguard the future of the United States.

Chapter 3: The Long-Term Consequences of Printing More American Dollars on the Value of the Currency

Understanding Currency Devaluation and Its Effects

In today's global economy, currency devaluation is a topic of great concern and interest to economists and the public alike. In this subchapter, we will delve into the intricacies of currency devaluation and its effects on various aspects of the US economy. Specifically, we will explore the impact of overspending and increased money supply on inflation rates, the role of foreign debt in exacerbating the US deficit crisis, the long-term consequences of printing more American dollars on the value of the currency, and the connection between overspending and income inequality in the US.

First and foremost, it is crucial to comprehend the relationship between overspending and inflation rates. When a government spends more than it generates in revenue, it often resorts to printing more money to cover the deficit. This injection of excess money into the economy leads to an increase in the money supply, which in turn fuels inflation. Consequently, the purchasing power of the currency diminishes, and prices for goods and services rise, eroding the wealth of individuals and businesses alike.

Foreign debt also plays a significant role in exacerbating the US deficit crisis. As the government accumulates more debt from foreign countries, it becomes increasingly vulnerable to economic shocks and fluctuations in interest rates. Moreover, the reliance on foreign financing can lead to a loss of economic independence and control over monetary policy, potentially compromising national interests.

The long-term consequences of printing more American dollars are equally concerning. This practice can undermine the value of the currency, reducing its purchasing power on the international stage. As the US dollar loses prestige, it becomes less desirable for foreign investors, which could result in a decline in foreign investment and a subsequent decrease in economic growth.

Furthermore, the connection between overspending and income inequality cannot be ignored. When the government focuses its spending on certain sectors or groups, it can exacerbate income disparities. This is particularly evident when the benefits of overspending primarily flow to the wealthy, leaving the majority of Americans struggling to make ends meet.

The economic implications of overspending and increased money supply extend beyond income inequality. Small businesses, for instance, face challenges as rising inflation erodes their profit margins and makes it more difficult to compete. Additionally, the US deficit has a direct impact on interest rates and borrowing costs. As the government borrows more to finance its spending, interest rates rise, making it costlier for individuals and businesses to borrow money, thereby slowing economic activity.

The relationship between overspending and the national debt is alarming, especially considering its impact on future generations. The burden of the national debt falls on young Americans, who will inherit a weakened economy and face the challenge of repaying their predecessors' excessive spending.

Moreover, overspending and increased money supply have implications beyond the domestic economy. As the US deficit grows, it can negatively affect global financial markets and international trade. The uncertainty surrounding the value of the US dollar and the stability of the economy can lead to volatile markets and hinder international trade relationships.

Finally, overspending and increased money supply have political implications as well. Government policies and decision-making can be influenced by the need to maintain economic stability, potentially compromising other priorities and goals.

In conclusion, understanding currency devaluation and its effects is crucial to grasp the potential risks and vulnerabilities of the US economy due to continuous overspending and printing more American dollars. From inflation rates to income inequality, international trade to political decision-making, the consequences of these practices are far-reaching and have the potential to shape the future of the nation. It is imperative for economists and the public to be aware of these issues and engage in informed discussions to ensure a more stable and resilient economy for generations to come.

The Implications of a Weaker US Dollar on Trade and Investments

In today's globalized economy, the strength of a country's currency plays a crucial role in determining its trade and investment prospects. A weaker currency, such as the US dollar, can have far-reaching implications that impact various aspects of the economy. This subchapter explores the implications of a weaker US dollar on trade and investments, shedding light on the potential risks and vulnerabilities that arise due to continuous overspending and printing more American dollars.

One of the immediate effects of a weaker US dollar is the impact on inflation rates. As the value of the currency declines, the cost of imported goods and commodities rises, leading to higher inflation. This can have a detrimental effect on the purchasing power of the public, especially those on fixed incomes or with limited resources.

The role of foreign debt in exacerbating the US deficit crisis cannot be ignored. A weaker currency makes it more expensive for the government to service its foreign debt, further exacerbating the deficit crisis. This can result in higher borrowing costs, which in turn burdens future generations with the responsibility of paying off the debt.

Furthermore, the long-term consequences of printing more American dollars on the value of the currency cannot be overlooked. Continuous overspending and money supply expansion can lead to a devaluation of the US dollar, eroding its purchasing power and diminishing its status as a global reserve currency.

Overspending and increased money supply also have a connection with income inequality in the US. The wealthy tend to have assets that appreciate in value during inflationary periods, while the less affluent struggle with rising prices and stagnant wages. This exacerbates the already existing income gap within the country.

Small businesses also bear the brunt of overspending and increased money supply. As the value of the currency declines, the cost of imported raw materials and components rises, making it difficult for small businesses to compete globally. This can have a detrimental effect on their growth and profitability.

The US deficit and its impact on interest rates and borrowing costs are closely intertwined. A larger deficit increases the supply of US treasuries, leading to higher interest rates and borrowing costs. This can dampen investments and hinder economic growth.

Moreover, overspending and increased money supply have implications for future generations. The growing national debt burdens future generations with the responsibility of paying off the debt and reduces their economic opportunities.

The influence of overspending on global financial markets and international trade cannot be underestimated. A weaker US dollar can make US exports more competitive, but it also makes imports more expensive. This can lead to trade imbalances and potential trade conflicts with other nations.

The political implications of overspending and increased money supply are significant. Governments may be tempted to continue overspending and printing more money to maintain short-term economic stability, but this can lead to long-term economic vulnerabilities and a loss of confidence in the currency.

In conclusion, the implications of a weaker US dollar on trade and investments are vast and multifaceted. Continuous overspending and printing more American dollars pose potential risks and vulnerabilities to the US economy. It is crucial for economists and the public to understand these implications to make informed decisions and shape policies that promote long-term economic stability and growth.

The Potential Threats to the US Dollar as the Reserve Currency

In recent years, there has been growing concern among economists and the public regarding the potential threats to the US dollar as the reserve currency. This subchapter aims to shed light on the various aspects of this issue, including the impact of overspending and increased money supply on inflation rates, the role of foreign debt in exacerbating the US deficit crisis, and the long-term consequences of printing more American dollars on the value of the currency.

One of the most significant threats to the US dollar as the reserve currency is the impact of overspending and increased money supply on inflation rates. As the government continues to spend beyond its means and print more money, it risks devaluing the currency and eroding its purchasing power. This not only affects the domestic economy but also has far-reaching implications for global markets and international trade.

Moreover, the role of foreign debt cannot be overlooked in exacerbating the US deficit crisis. As the government borrows more money from foreign countries to finance its spending, it becomes increasingly reliant on external sources. This not only puts the US economy at the mercy of foreign creditors but also raises concerns about the sustainability of the debt and its impact on future generations.

The long-term consequences of printing more American dollars are equally worrisome. As the supply of money increases, the value of the currency decreases. This can lead to higher inflation rates, reduced purchasing power, and a loss of confidence in the US dollar as a stable store of value. The ramifications of such a scenario are not only economic but also political, as it may influence government policies and decision-making.

Furthermore, overspending and increased money supply have been linked to income inequality in the US. As the government prioritizes certain sectors or individuals through its spending, it perpetuates a system that favors the wealthy and widens the gap between the rich and the poor. This has profound social implications and can further exacerbate economic disparities within the country.

Small businesses are also significantly affected by the economic implications of overspending and increased money supply. As inflation rises and the value of the currency decreases, the cost of goods and services increases, making it harder for small businesses to compete. This can stifle entrepreneurship, hinder economic growth, and lead to job losses.

In addition, the US deficit has a direct impact on interest rates and borrowing costs. As the government borrows more money to finance its spending, it puts upward pressure on interest rates, making it more expensive for businesses and individuals to borrow. This can dampen investment, reduce consumer spending, and hinder economic recovery.

Ultimately, the potential risks and vulnerabilities of the US economy due to continuous overspending and printing more American dollars are far-reaching. They extend beyond domestic concerns and have profound implications for global financial markets, international trade, and government policies. It is crucial for economists and the public to understand these threats and work towards sustainable economic practices to protect the stability of the US dollar as the reserve currency.

Chapter 4: The Connection Between Overspending and Income Inequality in the US

The Relationship Between Government Policies and Income Distribution

In today's economic landscape, it is crucial to understand the intricate relationship between government policies and income distribution. This subchapter explores the various dimensions of this relationship, shedding light on the potential risks and vulnerabilities of the US economy due to continuous overspending and printing more American dollars. Addressed to economists and the public, this analysis aims to provide a comprehensive understanding of the impact of government policies on income distribution and its wider implications.

One of the key areas of examination in this subchapter is the impact of overspending and increased money supply on inflation rates. By delving into the consequences of excessive government spending and the subsequent rise in the money supply, economists and the public can grasp the intricate dynamics between these factors and the resultant inflation rates.

Furthermore, this subchapter explores the role of foreign debt in exacerbating the US deficit crisis. By understanding how foreign debt influences the deficit, economists and the public can gain insights into the broader implications for income distribution and the overall stability of the economy.

The long-term consequences of printing more American dollars on the value of the currency are also analyzed. By examining the potential risks and vulnerabilities associated with the continuous printing of dollars, economists and the public can better comprehend the potential impact on income distribution and the value of the currency in the long run.

Moreover, the connection between overspending and income inequality in the US is explored in this subchapter. By examining the economic implications of overspending and increased money supply on small businesses, economists and the public can gain a deeper understanding of the distributional effects of government policies on income.

Additionally, this subchapter delves into the effect of the US deficit on interest rates and borrowing costs. By understanding the relationship between overspending and the national debt and its impact on future generations, economists and the public can appreciate the long-term consequences of government policies on income distribution.

Furthermore, the influence of overspending on global financial markets and international trade is examined. By understanding the implications of government policies on income distribution, economists and the public can appreciate the wider implications for global economic stability.

Lastly, this subchapter analyzes the political implications of overspending and increased money supply on government policies and decision-making. By understanding the potential risks and vulnerabilities of the US economy due to continuous overspending and printing more American dollars, economists and the public can better evaluate the consequences for income distribution and make informed decisions.

In conclusion, this subchapter provides a comprehensive analysis of the relationship between government policies and income distribution in the context of continuous overspending and printing more American dollars. By examining the impact on inflation rates, foreign debt, currency value, income inequality, small businesses, interest rates, national debt, global financial markets, international trade, and political decision-making, economists and the public can gain a holistic understanding of the potential risks and vulnerabilities of the US economy.

The Impact of Wealth Concentration on Economic Stability

Wealth concentration, the unequal distribution of wealth within a society, has far-reaching implications on economic stability. In this subchapter, we will explore how the concentration of wealth affects various aspects of the US economy, shedding light on the potential risks and vulnerabilities that arise due to continuous overspending and printing more American dollars.

One of the key consequences of wealth concentration is the exacerbation of income inequality. As a result of overspending and increased money supply, the rich tend to become richer while the poor struggle to make ends meet. This disparity not only undermines social cohesion but also hampers economic growth. Studies have shown that high levels of income inequality can limit economic mobility and hinder long-term prosperity.

Moreover, wealth concentration has a direct impact on small businesses. As wealth becomes concentrated in the hands of a few, access to capital becomes more limited for entrepreneurs and small enterprises. This lack of financial resources stifles innovation and hampers job creation, ultimately compromising the overall health of the economy.

The US deficit crisis is further exacerbated by the role of foreign debt. Overspending and increased money supply have led to a ballooning deficit, which is largely financed through borrowing from foreign countries. This reliance on foreign debt not only increases the vulnerability of the US economy but also exposes it to potential economic shocks from abroad.

The consequence of printing more American dollars is the devaluation of the currency. As the money supply increases, the value of the dollar decreases, leading to inflation. This erosion of purchasing power affects all individuals, particularly those with limited financial resources. It also dampens investor confidence, both domestically and internationally, and undermines the stability of financial markets.

Furthermore, the continuous overspending and printing of more American dollars have significant long-term consequences. The national debt, already at unprecedented levels, burdens future generations with increasing interest payments and limited fiscal flexibility. This intergenerational inequity not only undermines economic stability but also restricts the ability of future policymakers to address pressing societal needs.

The political implications of overspending and increased money supply are also noteworthy. Government policies and decision-making become increasingly influenced by the need to finance the deficit, often resulting in short-term fixes that fail to address the root causes of economic challenges. This reliance on unsustainable fiscal practices compromises the ability of policymakers to implement long-term solutions and undermines public trust in government institutions.

Finally, the impact of overspending and increased money supply extends beyond domestic borders. The US economy's vulnerabilities have global repercussions, affecting international trade and financial markets. As the largest economy in the world, any instability in the US economy reverberates across the globe, potentially triggering economic crises in other countries.

In conclusion, wealth concentration has a profound impact on economic stability. The consequences of overspending and printing more American dollars are vast, affecting inflation rates, income inequality, small businesses, interest rates, borrowing costs, global financial markets, international trade, government policies, and future generations. It is crucial for economists and the public to understand these potential risks and vulnerabilities to foster a sustainable and resilient US economy.

The Role of Education and Social Mobility in Reducing Income Inequality

Income inequality has become a pressing issue in the United States, with the gap between the rich and the poor widening over the years. In order to address this issue, it is crucial to understand the role of education and social mobility in reducing income inequality.

Education plays a vital role in providing individuals with the necessary skills and knowledge to succeed in the workforce. A well-educated workforce is more likely to earn higher wages, have better job prospects, and contribute to economic growth. However, access to quality education is not evenly distributed, with disadvantaged communities often lacking the resources and opportunities needed to obtain a good education.

By investing in education, policymakers can help level the playing field and provide equal opportunities for all individuals. This includes improving access to early childhood education, enhancing the quality of K-12 schools in low-income areas, and expanding affordable higher education options. Additionally, providing financial aid and scholarships to students from disadvantaged backgrounds can help mitigate the financial barriers that often prevent them from pursuing higher education.

Furthermore, social mobility plays a crucial role in reducing income inequality. Social mobility refers to the ability of individuals to move up the economic ladder based on their own merit and hard work. However, in the current system, social mobility is often limited, with individuals from lower-income backgrounds facing significant barriers to upward mobility.

To address this issue, it is important to implement policies that promote social mobility. This includes providing job training and skills development programs for individuals in low-income communities, creating pathways for career advancement, and implementing policies that ensure equal pay for equal work. Additionally, addressing systemic issues such as discrimination and inequality in the workplace can also contribute to increasing social mobility.

By investing in education and promoting social mobility, policymakers can help reduce income inequality in the United States. These measures not only provide individuals with the tools they need to succeed but also contribute to a more equitable and inclusive society. It is crucial that policymakers prioritize these issues and work towards creating a system that provides equal opportunities for all individuals, regardless of their socio-economic background.

Overall, education and social mobility play a crucial role in reducing income inequality. By investing in these areas, policymakers can help create a more equitable society and ensure that all individuals have the opportunity to succeed and contribute to the economy. It is imperative that economists and the public understand the importance of these factors in addressing income inequality, as they are key to creating a sustainable and inclusive economy for future generations.

Chapter 5: The Economic Implications of Overspending and Increased Money Supply on Small Businesses

The Challenges Faced by Small Businesses in an Inflationary Environment

Inflation is a persistent increase in the general price level of goods and services in an economy over time. In an inflationary environment, small businesses face numerous challenges that can significantly impact their operations and sustainability. This subchapter explores the various obstacles encountered by small businesses in such an environment and the implications for the broader US economy.

One of the primary challenges small businesses face in an inflationary environment is the rising cost of inputs. As prices of raw materials, energy, and labor increase, small businesses find it increasingly difficult to maintain their profit margins. This can lead to higher production costs and, in turn, higher prices for consumers, potentially reducing demand for their products or services.

Moreover, small businesses often lack the bargaining power of larger corporations when negotiating with suppliers. As a result, they bear the brunt of price increases, putting them at a competitive disadvantage. This can lead to reduced market share and, in some cases, business closures.

The connection between overspending and increased money supply and its impact on inflation rates becomes particularly relevant for small businesses. Government overspending and the subsequent increase in the money supply can significantly contribute to inflation. When the purchasing power of the currency erodes, small businesses struggle to maintain stable prices and profitability.

Another challenge for small businesses in an inflationary environment is the potential impact on borrowing costs. As inflation rises, central banks often respond by increasing interest rates to curb inflationary pressures. This, in turn, leads to higher borrowing costs for small businesses, limiting their access to capital for expansion or investment.

Furthermore, the economic implications of overspending and increased money supply also contribute to income inequality. Small businesses, particularly those in low-income communities, often lack the resources to cope with inflationary pressures, exacerbating the wealth gap. This can have long-term consequences for both the affected businesses and the overall economy.

In conclusion, small businesses face numerous challenges in an inflationary environment. Rising input costs, reduced market share, limited access to capital, and increased income inequality are just a few of the obstacles they must navigate. Understanding these challenges is crucial for economists and the public to recognize the potential risks and vulnerabilities of the US economy due to continuous overspending and printing more American dollars. Small businesses play a vital role in the economy, and addressing their challenges in an inflationary environment is essential for sustainable economic growth and prosperity.

The Effect of Rising Interest Rates on Small Business Loans

In the complex web of the US economy, the interplay between interest rates and small business loans is a crucial factor that cannot be overlooked. As interest rates rise, the impact on small businesses becomes increasingly pronounced, affecting their ability to secure funding and ultimately impacting economic growth. This subchapter aims to explore the multifaceted effects of rising interest rates on small business loans, shedding light on the consequences that economists and the public should be aware of.

When interest rates increase, borrowing costs for small businesses surge, making it more challenging for them to access the capital they need to grow and expand their operations. As a result, these businesses may be forced to delay investments, reduce hiring, or even halt their expansion plans altogether. This not only stifles innovation and entrepreneurship but also hampers job creation and economic development.

Furthermore, the connection between rising interest rates and the US deficit crisis cannot be ignored. As the government spends more than it collects in revenue, it must borrow money, leading to an increase in the national debt. This mounting debt, coupled with rising interest rates, places upward pressure on borrowing costs for businesses. Consequently, small businesses face higher interest payments on existing loans and encounter greater difficulty in obtaining new financing.

The impact of rising interest rates on small business loans extends beyond the domestic realm. With the US economy being interconnected with global financial markets, any turbulence caused by increased borrowing costs can reverberate across international borders. As small businesses face higher interest rates, they may struggle to compete in the global marketplace, hindering international trade and potentially leading to a decline in exports.

Moreover, the long-term consequences of rising interest rates on small business loans can have a ripple effect on income inequality. As small businesses face higher borrowing costs, they may struggle to generate sufficient revenue to provide competitive wages and benefits to their employees. This exacerbates income inequality, threatening social and economic stability.

In conclusion, the effect of rising interest rates on small business loans is a critical issue that economists and the public must grapple with. The implications range from stunted economic growth and job creation to exacerbating income inequality and hindering international trade. As the

US economy continues to grapple with the risks and vulnerabilities of continuous overspending and the printing of more American dollars, finding solutions to mitigate the impact of rising interest rates on small business loans becomes imperative to foster a resilient and inclusive economy.

Strategies for Small Businesses to Navigate Economic Uncertainty

In today's economic landscape, small businesses face numerous challenges due to economic uncertainty caused by overspending and increased money supply. As economists and the public grapple with the potential risks and vulnerabilities of the US economy, it is crucial for small businesses to adopt effective strategies to navigate these uncertain times. Here are some key strategies for small businesses to consider:

1. Diversify your customer base: In times of economic uncertainty, it is essential to diversify your customer base to reduce dependence on a single market segment. By expanding your customer reach, you can mitigate the impact of fluctuations in demand and reduce the risk of revenue loss.

2. Monitor inflation rates: Small businesses must closely monitor inflation rates as they directly influence the cost of goods and services. By staying informed about inflation trends, businesses can adjust their pricing strategies and manage their expenses effectively.

3. Optimize cash flow management: Maintaining a healthy cash flow is crucial during economic uncertainty. Small businesses should focus on reducing unnecessary expenses, negotiating favorable payment terms with suppliers, and ensuring timely invoice collections to improve their cash flow position.

4. Seek government assistance: Small businesses should explore available government assistance programs and grants to alleviate the financial burden caused by economic uncertainty. These programs can provide

access to capital, training, and resources that can help businesses weather the storm.

5. Embrace technology and innovation: In times of economic uncertainty, businesses that embrace technology and innovation tend to fare better. Small businesses should leverage digital platforms, e-commerce, and automation to streamline operations, reach new markets, and drive efficiency.

6. Build strong relationships with suppliers and customers: Maintaining strong relationships with suppliers and customers is vital during economic uncertainty. By fostering trust and open communication, businesses can negotiate favorable terms, collaborate on cost-saving initiatives, and adapt to changing market dynamics together.

7. Stay agile and adaptable: Economic uncertainty often calls for quick decision-making and adaptability. Small businesses should regularly evaluate their business strategies, identify new opportunities, and be willing to pivot when necessary to stay ahead of the curve.

By implementing these strategies, small businesses can navigate economic uncertainty caused by overspending and increased money supply. While the potential risks and vulnerabilities of the US economy persist, businesses that proactively respond to these challenges will increase their chances of survival and long-term success.

Chapter 6: The Effect of the US Deficit on Interest Rates and Borrowing Costs

The Relationship Between Government Borrowing and Interest Rates

In today's economic landscape, the relationship between government borrowing and interest rates is a topic of paramount importance. As economists and the public grapple with the impact of overspending and increased money supply on various aspects of the US economy, understanding this connection becomes crucial. This subchapter aims to shed light on this intricate relationship and its implications for both economists and the general public.

One key consequence of overspending and increased money supply is its effect on inflation rates. When the government overspends and prints more American dollars, it floods the market with excess money, leading to an increase in prices. This inflationary pressure erodes the purchasing power of individuals and poses a challenge for economists in maintaining price stability.

Foreign debt plays an essential role in exacerbating the US deficit crisis. As the government borrows from foreign entities to finance its spending, it further deepens the deficit, leading to a vicious cycle of increasing debt burdens. This has long-term consequences for the value of the US currency, as excessive borrowing weakens the dollar and erodes its standing in global markets.

Moreover, overspending and increased money supply have a direct connection to income inequality in the US. As the government allocates resources to fund its spending, it often neglects investments in social welfare programs and infrastructure. This exacerbates the income gap, leaving the most vulnerable segments of society at a significant disadvantage.

The economic implications of overspending and increased money supply also extend to small businesses. As interest rates rise due to the government's borrowing, small businesses face higher borrowing costs, making it increasingly challenging to secure financing for growth and expansion. This hinders innovation and job creation, further hampering economic progress.

Furthermore, the US deficit influences interest rates and borrowing costs. As the government accumulates debt, it competes with private borrowers for available funds, driving up interest rates. This not only impacts the government's ability to service its debt but also affects the affordability of borrowing for businesses and individuals.

The impact of overspending and increased money supply on future generations cannot be overlooked. The growing national debt, fueled by continuous overspending, burdens future generations with the responsibility of repaying these obligations. This can hinder their economic prospects and limit their ability to invest in vital areas such as education and infrastructure.

The influence of overspending on global financial markets and international trade cannot be underestimated. Excessive borrowing by the US government can lead to a loss of confidence in the US economy, causing investors to withdraw their funds and destabilizing global financial markets. Additionally, it can strain international trade relationships, as the US's ability to repay its debts may be called into question.

The political implications of overspending and increased money supply are significant, as they shape government policies and decision-making. The pursuit of short-term political gains often drives governments to overspend, leading to a cycle of continuous deficits. This compromises the long-term stability and sustainability of the economy.

In conclusion, the potential risks and vulnerabilities of the US economy due to continuous overspending and printing more American dollars are manifold. The relationship between government borrowing and interest rates is a critical aspect of this discussion, with implications for inflation rates, income inequality, small businesses, future generations, global financial markets, and government policies. It is crucial for economists and the public to grapple with these issues to ensure the long-term stability and prosperity of the US economy.

The Impact of Higher Interest Rates on Borrowers and Investors

In the ongoing discussion about the potential risks and vulnerabilities of the US economy due to continuous overspending and printing more American dollars, one crucial aspect that cannot be overlooked is the impact of higher interest rates on both borrowers and investors. This subchapter delves into the consequences that arise when interest rates rise as a result of unsustainable fiscal policies.

For borrowers, higher interest rates mean increased borrowing costs. Whether it's a small business seeking funds for expansion or an individual applying for a mortgage, the cost of borrowing becomes more expensive as interest rates climb. This can lead to a decrease in consumer spending and investment, which ultimately hampers economic growth. Additionally, higher interest rates can make it harder for borrowers to repay their existing debts, potentially leading to a rise in default rates and financial instability.

On the other hand, investors face their own set of challenges when interest rates rise. Fixed-income investments such as bonds become more attractive as they offer higher yields. This can result in a shift of investments from riskier assets like stocks to safer fixed-income instruments. The stock market may experience a decline as investors reallocate their portfolios, leading to increased volatility and potential wealth erosion. Moreover, higher interest rates can reduce the present value of future cash flows, impacting the valuation of various investment assets.

The connection between higher interest rates and the national debt cannot be ignored. As the government continues to overspend and accumulate debt, the pressure to finance this debt increases. To attract investors, the government must offer higher interest rates on newly issued bonds. This, in turn, raises borrowing costs for the government and increases the burden on future generations, who will have to shoulder the responsibility of paying off the mounting debt.

Furthermore, higher interest rates have implications for global financial markets and international trade. As the US borrowing costs increase, it becomes more expensive for foreign investors to finance the US deficit. This can lead to a reduction in foreign demand for US assets, potentially weakening the value of the US dollar and negatively impacting international trade relationships.

The potential risks and vulnerabilities of the US economy due to continuous overspending and printing more American dollars are vast. The impact of higher interest rates on borrowers and investors is just one aspect of the complex web of consequences that arise from unsustainable fiscal policies. Economists and the public must thoroughly understand these implications to foster informed discussions and push for responsible economic decision-making.

The Role of the Federal Reserve in Managing Interest Rates

In the intricate web of the US economy, one institution stands out for its pivotal role in managing interest rates - the Federal Reserve. This subchapter explores how the Federal Reserve wields its power to control interest rates and the implications it carries for various sectors of the economy.

Interest rates have far-reaching effects, influencing everything from inflation rates to borrowing costs and income inequality. The Federal Reserve, as the central banking system of the United States, plays a crucial role in managing these rates through its monetary policy tools.

One of the primary tools employed by the Federal Reserve to manage interest rates is the buying and selling of government securities in the open market. By purchasing government bonds, the Federal Reserve increases the money supply, lowering interest rates. Conversely, by selling these securities, they reduce the money supply, increasing interest rates. This mechanism allows the Federal Reserve to influence borrowing costs and stimulate or restrain economic growth accordingly.

The impact of overspending and increased money supply on inflation rates is a critical concern. The Federal Reserve closely monitors inflation and adjusts interest rates to maintain price stability. By managing interest rates, they aim to control inflation and prevent it from eroding the value of the currency.

Foreign debt also plays a role in exacerbating the US deficit crisis. As the Federal Reserve manages interest rates, it indirectly affects the costs of servicing foreign debt. Higher interest rates can inflate these costs, posing a challenge for the US economy.

The consequences of printing more American dollars on the value of the currency are significant. Excessive money supply can lead to a devaluation of the currency, eroding its purchasing power. The Federal Reserve's role involves maintaining a delicate balance to prevent such risks while fostering economic growth.

Overspending and increased money supply have a connection to income inequality in the US. The Federal Reserve's management of interest rates can impact small businesses, affecting their borrowing costs and ability to thrive. By understanding this connection, policymakers can work towards a more equitable economic landscape.

The US deficit and its impact on interest rates and borrowing costs are closely intertwined. Overspending and increased money supply can strain the deficit, leading to higher interest rates and borrowing costs. The Federal Reserve's role becomes crucial in managing these rates to ensure sustainable economic growth.

Furthermore, overspending and increased money supply have long-term implications for future generations. The accumulation of national debt due to continuous overspending burdens future generations with the obligation to repay. The Federal Reserve's role in managing interest rates affects the magnitude of this burden.

Overspending and increased money supply also have global implications. The value of the US dollar influences global financial markets and international trade. The Federal Reserve's actions in managing interest rates can ripple through these markets, impacting economies worldwide.

The political implications of overspending and increased money supply on government policies and decision-making are profound. The Federal Reserve's role is not immune to political pressures, which can influence its decisions and actions. Understanding these implications is crucial for policymakers and the public.

This subchapter sheds light on the potential risks and vulnerabilities of the US economy due to continuous overspending and printing more American dollars. The Federal Reserve's role in managing interest rates is a critical component in addressing these risks and fostering economic stability and growth. Economists and the public must comprehend the intricacies of this role to navigate the challenges and opportunities that lie ahead.

Chapter 7: The Relationship Between Overspending and the National Debt, and Its Impact on Future Generations

Understanding the National Debt and Its Components

In the quest to unravel the complexities of the US economy, it is crucial to comprehend the national debt and its components. This subchapter aims to shed light on this crucial topic, addressing economists and the public alike.

One of the key concerns surrounding overspending and increased money supply is its impact on inflation rates. As the government injects more money into the economy, there is a risk of the value of the currency decreasing, leading to higher prices for goods and services. This can have severe consequences for individuals and businesses alike.

Foreign debt plays a significant role in exacerbating the US deficit crisis. As the government borrows from foreign nations, it further adds to the burden of the national debt. This dependency on external sources poses risks and vulnerabilities to the US economy, as it becomes susceptible to the decisions and policies of other nations.

Printing more American dollars, a response often used to alleviate economic challenges, can have long-term consequences. The value of the currency can depreciate, impacting the purchasing power of individuals and businesses. Moreover, this can lead to a loss of confidence in the US dollar, affecting its status as the global reserve currency.

Overspending has also been linked to income inequality in the US. As the government channels funds disproportionately, the gap between the wealthy and the rest of society widens. This has implications for social stability and economic growth, as a more equitable distribution of resources is essential for a sustainable economy.

Small businesses bear the brunt of overspending and increased money supply. The economic implications are vast, as these businesses struggle with rising costs and increased competition. This can hinder their growth and innovation, ultimately impacting job creation and economic prosperity.

The US deficit also has a direct effect on interest rates and borrowing costs. As the government borrows to finance its overspending, it competes with other borrowers, driving up interest rates. This, in turn, increases the cost of borrowing for individuals, businesses, and the government itself.

The connection between overspending and the national debt must not be overlooked, as it has a profound impact on future generations. The burden of the national debt falls on the shoulders of the next generation, limiting their opportunities and economic mobility.

Overspending also reverberates in global financial markets and international trade. The US economy's actions have far-reaching consequences, affecting the stability of the global financial system and influencing trade relationships with other nations.

Lastly, the political implications of overspending and increased money supply are significant. Government policies and decision-making are heavily influenced by the need to address the economic challenges stemming from continuous overspending. This can have implications for the overall governance and effectiveness of public policies.

In conclusion, understanding the national debt and its components is crucial to grasp the potential risks and vulnerabilities of the US economy. Overspending and increased money supply have implications for inflation rates, income inequality, small businesses, interest rates, global financial markets, international trade, and government policies. It is imperative that economists and the public alike comprehend these complexities to make informed decisions and contribute to a more sustainable economic future.

The Burden of Debt on Future Generations

Title: The Burden of Debt on Future Generations: Understanding the Consequences of Continuous Overspending and Money Printing

Introduction:

In the book "Fragile Foundations: The Potential Risks and Vulnerabilities of the US Economy Due to Continuous Overspending and Printing More American Dollars," we delve into the critical issue of the burden of debt on future generations. This subchapter aims to address economists and the public, shedding light on the far-reaching consequences of continuous overspending and increased money supply.

The Impact of Overspending and Increased Money Supply on Inflation Rates:

One of the primary concerns arising from overspending and monetary expansion is the impact on inflation rates. Excessive government expenditures and an increase in the money supply can lead to a surge in prices, eroding the purchasing power of citizens and hindering economic stability.

The Role of Foreign Debt in Exacerbating the US Deficit Crisis:

Foreign debt plays a crucial role in exacerbating the US deficit crisis. As the government borrows from foreign entities, it becomes increasingly dependent on their goodwill, subjecting the economy to potential risks and vulnerabilities.

The Long-term Consequences of Printing More American Dollars on Currency Value:

Printing more American dollars devalues the currency and poses long-term consequences. A weakened currency reduces the country's international competitiveness, impacting trade, investment, and ultimately affecting the economic well-being of future generations.

The Connection Between Overspending and Income Inequality:

Overspending exacerbates income inequality in the US. As government resources are disproportionately allocated, the gap between the rich and the poor widens, leading to social unrest and economic instability.

The Economic Implications of Overspending on Small Businesses:

Continuous overspending and increased money supply have adverse economic implications on small businesses. It leads to rising interest rates, reduced access to credit, and increased operating costs, making it harder for small businesses to survive and thrive.

The Effect of the US Deficit on Interest Rates and Borrowing Costs:

The US deficit impacts interest rates and borrowing costs. As the government borrows more to finance its overspending, it competes with private borrowers, driving up interest rates and increasing the cost of borrowing for future generations.

The Relationship Between Overspending, National Debt, and Its Impact on Future Generations:

Overspending contributes to the national debt, leaving a burden on future generations. As the debt accumulates, it limits the government's ability to invest in vital areas such as education, healthcare, and infrastructure, hindering economic growth and prosperity.

The Influence of Overspending on Global Financial Markets and International Trade:

Overspending and increased money supply in the US can have a significant impact on global financial markets and international trade. Fluctuating exchange rates, trade imbalances, and market volatility are some of the consequences that can affect the livelihoods of future generations.

The Political Implications of Overspending on Government Policies and Decision-Making:

Overspending and monetary expansion have profound political implications. It can lead to short-term policy decisions aimed at appeasing voters, but with long-term consequences that burden future generations with unmanageable debt.

The Potential Risks and Vulnerabilities of the US Economy Due to Continuous Overspending and Money Printing:

Continuous overspending and money printing expose the US economy to potential risks and vulnerabilities. These include hyperinflation, reduced investor confidence, and a weakened economy that future generations will inherit.

Conclusion:

Understanding the burden of debt on future generations is vital for economists and the public alike. By acknowledging the impact of overspending and increased money supply on inflation rates, income inequality, currency value, small businesses, interest rates, and the national debt, we can work towards ensuring a more sustainable and prosperous future for generations to come.

Potential Solutions to Reduce the National Debt

The national debt of the United States has reached unprecedented levels, posing significant risks and vulnerabilities to the economy. In order to address this pressing issue, it is essential to explore potential solutions that can effectively reduce the national debt. This subchapter aims to present a comprehensive analysis of various strategies that can be adopted to tackle this crisis.

One potential solution is to implement fiscal discipline and reduce government spending. By cutting unnecessary expenditures and streamlining government programs, the deficit can be reduced significantly. This approach requires tough decisions and political will, but it is crucial to ensure the long-term sustainability of the economy.

Another approach to reduce the national debt is to increase revenues through tax reform. By simplifying the tax code and closing loopholes, the government can generate additional revenue without burdening the middle and lower-income households. This can help in reducing the deficit while ensuring a fair distribution of the tax burden.

Furthermore, addressing income inequality can play a crucial role in reducing the national debt. Policies that promote inclusive economic growth and provide equal opportunities for all citizens can help in narrowing the income gap. This, in turn, can lead to higher tax revenues and reduce the need for excessive borrowing.

In addition, the government should consider negotiating and restructuring foreign debt to alleviate the deficit crisis. By engaging in diplomatic efforts and renegotiating terms with foreign creditors, the burden of foreign debt can be reduced, providing some relief to the economy.

Moreover, it is essential to focus on promoting economic growth and supporting small businesses. Small businesses are the backbone of the economy, and by providing them with necessary resources and incentives, they can contribute significantly to reducing the national debt. This can be achieved through targeted policies such as tax incentives, access to capital, and streamlined regulatory processes.

Lastly, the government should prioritize long-term planning and make informed decisions regarding spending and borrowing. By considering the impact on future generations, policymakers can adopt a responsible approach that ensures sustainable economic growth and reduces the burden on future taxpayers.

In conclusion, reducing the national debt requires a multi-faceted approach that includes fiscal discipline, tax reform, addressing income inequality, restructuring foreign debt, supporting small businesses, and long-term planning. These potential solutions, if implemented effectively, can help in mitigating the risks and vulnerabilities posed by continuous overspending and the printing of more American dollars. It is imperative for economists and the public to engage in a constructive dialogue and advocate for these solutions to secure the future of the US economy.

Chapter 8: The Influence of Overspending on Global Financial Markets and International Trade

The Spillover Effects of US Economic Policies on Global Markets

In today's interconnected world, the policies and actions of major economies can have far-reaching consequences on global markets. The United States, as the largest economy in the world, holds a significant role in shaping the international economic landscape. This subchapter explores the spillover effects of US economic policies on global markets, shedding light on various aspects of this intricate relationship.

First and foremost, overspending and the increased money supply have a profound impact on inflation rates. As the US government continues to inject more money into the economy, the excess liquidity can lead to rising prices, eroding the purchasing power of individuals and businesses alike. This inflationary pressure extends beyond US borders, affecting other countries through the transmission of higher import prices and increased volatility in global commodity markets.

Moreover, foreign debt exacerbates the US deficit crisis, creating a vicious cycle of borrowing. As the US government accumulates more debt from foreign creditors, it becomes increasingly reliant on their willingness to finance its deficits. This vulnerability exposes the US economy to potential risks, as any sudden loss of confidence from foreign investors could trigger a severe financial crisis.

Another crucial concern is the long-term consequences of printing more American dollars on the value of the currency. As the money supply expands, the value of the dollar can depreciate, affecting international trade and investment. This depreciation can make US exports more competitive but also increase the cost of imported goods, potentially leading to trade imbalances and protectionist measures from other countries.

The connection between overspending and income inequality in the US cannot be ignored. As the government allocates more resources towards public spending, the burden of taxation falls disproportionately on certain segments of society. This exacerbates income inequality, leading to social tensions and potential economic instability.

Additionally, the implications of overspending and increased money supply on small businesses are significant. These entities often struggle to cope with rising costs and increased competition, hindering their growth and job creation potential. Therefore, it is crucial to address these challenges through targeted policies that support the development and resilience of small businesses.

The US deficit also has implications for interest rates and borrowing costs. As the government competes for funds in the capital markets, it drives up interest rates, making it more expensive for businesses and individuals to borrow. This can dampen investment and consumption, curbing economic growth both domestically and globally.

Furthermore, overspending and the national debt have long-term consequences for future generations. The accumulation of debt places a burden on future taxpayers who will have to bear the costs of servicing and repaying it. This intergenerational transfer of liabilities raises ethical questions about the sustainability of current fiscal policies.

The influence of US overspending on global financial markets and international trade is undeniable. As the US economy experiences fluctuations and imbalances, these reverberate across the globe, affecting exchange rates, stock markets, and investor sentiment. The interconnectedness of financial systems makes it crucial for policymakers to consider the potential spillover effects when formulating economic policies.

The political implications of overspending and increased money supply are also noteworthy. These policies can influence government decisions and shape the political landscape, as they are often subject to public scrutiny and debate. The effects can range from changes in political leadership to shifts in public sentiment and preferences.

Finally, continuous overspending and printing more American dollars pose potential risks and vulnerabilities to the US economy. These actions can lead to a loss of confidence in the currency, higher borrowing costs, and reduced economic competitiveness. It is essential to closely monitor and address these risks to ensure the stability and resilience of the US economy.

In conclusion, the spillover effects of US economic policies on global markets are far-reaching and multifaceted. From inflation rates to income inequality, small businesses to international trade, interest rates to political decision-making, the implications of overspending and increased money supply are extensive. Recognizing these connections is vital for economists and the public alike, as it allows for a deeper understanding of the potential risks and vulnerabilities that the US economy faces. By addressing these issues and implementing prudent policies, it is possible to build a more stable and sustainable economic future.

The Trade Imbalances Caused by Overspending

In recent years, the United States has faced a growing concern over its trade imbalances, a problem that can be largely attributed to the country's persistent overspending. This subchapter aims to shed light on the far-reaching implications of overspending and the subsequent increase in money supply on various aspects of the economy, both domestically and internationally.

One of the immediate consequences of overspending and increased money supply is the impact on inflation rates. As the government continues to spend more than it generates in revenue, it inevitably leads to a surge in the money supply. This excess liquidity in the economy fuels inflation, driving up prices and eroding the purchasing power of the dollar. Economists have long argued that an increase in money supply without a corresponding increase in goods and services leads to higher inflation rates.

Furthermore, the role of foreign debt cannot be overlooked when analyzing the US deficit crisis. As the government consistently borrows from foreign nations to finance its excessive spending, the national debt continues to skyrocket. This growing debt burden exacerbates the trade imbalances, as the US becomes increasingly reliant on imports to meet its domestic consumption needs. The trade deficit widens, causing a ripple effect on the economy and posing severe risks to its stability.

Another consequence of overspending and increased money supply is the long-term impact on the value of the currency. As more dollars are pumped into the economy, the value of each individual dollar diminishes. This depreciation not only affects the purchasing power of individuals and businesses but also undermines the attractiveness of the US dollar as a global reserve currency.

Moreover, overspending has been closely linked to income inequality in the United States. As the government allocates more resources towards certain sectors or programs, it inadvertently contributes to the concentration of wealth in the hands of a few. This growing income disparity not only raises social and political concerns but also has economic implications, as it affects consumer spending patterns and overall economic growth.

Small businesses, which are the backbone of the US economy, also bear the brunt of overspending and increased money supply. The inflationary pressures resulting from excessive government spending erode their profit margins and erode their ability to compete both domestically and internationally.

The US deficit also has a direct impact on interest rates and borrowing costs. As the government accumulates more debt, it needs to entice investors with higher interest rates, which in turn raises borrowing costs for businesses and individuals. This hampers investment and stifles economic growth in the long run.

Furthermore, the trade imbalances caused by overspending and increased money supply have profound implications for future generations. The mounting national debt burdens future taxpayers, limiting their ability to invest in education, infrastructure, and social programs. This intergenerational transfer of debt poses significant risks to the country's long-term economic stability.

The influence of overspending extends beyond national borders, impacting global financial markets and international trade. As the US economy faces mounting vulnerabilities, it has the potential to trigger global financial crises and disrupt international trade flows, affecting economies around the world.

Finally, overspending and increased money supply have significant political implications. The government's policies and decision-making processes are heavily influenced by the need to address the economic consequences of overspending. This can lead to short-term fixes, populist measures, and a lack of long-term planning, ultimately jeopardizing the country's economic well-being.

In conclusion, the trade imbalances caused by overspending and increased money supply pose severe risks and vulnerabilities to the US economy. From inflation rates and income inequality to the national debt and global financial markets, the consequences of continuous overspending and printing more American dollars are far-reaching. As economists and the public, it is crucial to recognize these risks and work towards more sustainable and responsible fiscal policies to safeguard the future of the US economy.

The Role of International Organizations in Addressing Global Economic Challenges

The global economic landscape is constantly evolving, presenting numerous challenges that require collective action and cooperation among nations. International organizations play a crucial role in addressing these challenges and finding sustainable solutions. In the context of the United States' continuous overspending and the printing of more American dollars, these organizations have become increasingly significant in mitigating potential risks and vulnerabilities to the US economy.

One of the key areas impacted by overspending and increased money supply is inflation rates. International organizations, such as the International Monetary Fund (IMF) and the World Bank, closely monitor and analyze the effects of these practices on inflation. By providing guidance and recommendations, they assist in maintaining stable inflation rates and preventing hyperinflation, which can have detrimental effects on the economy.

Furthermore, the role of foreign debt in exacerbating the US deficit crisis cannot be overlooked. Organizations like the Organization for Economic Cooperation and Development (OECD) and the G20 work towards ensuring responsible lending practices and debt management. Their oversight and assistance help prevent the accumulation of unsustainable levels of foreign debt, which can further compound the deficit crisis.

The long-term consequences of printing more American dollars on the value of the currency are also a concern. International organizations, such as the Bank for International Settlements (BIS), provide expertise in currency management and exchange rate stability. Through their research and policy recommendations, they help mitigate the potential devaluation of the US dollar, protecting its standing as a global reserve currency.

Overspending has direct implications on income inequality in the US. International organizations, like the United Nations (UN) and the Organization for Economic Cooperation and Development (OECD), work towards promoting inclusive economic growth and reducing income disparities. They highlight the connection between overspending and income inequality, urging governments to adopt policies that address this issue and ensure fair distribution of wealth.

Small businesses are particularly vulnerable to the economic implications of overspending and increased money supply. International organizations, such as the World Trade Organization (WTO) and the International Trade Centre (ITC), support small businesses by promoting fair trade practices and providing technical assistance. By advocating for a level playing field and access to global markets, they aim to mitigate the negative impact of overspending on small businesses.

The US deficit also has an impact on interest rates and borrowing costs. International organizations, including the Bank for International Settlements (BIS) and the Federal Reserve, collaborate to ensure stable interest rates and manage borrowing costs. Their coordination helps prevent excessive borrowing costs that can burden the economy and hinder economic growth.

The relationship between overspending and the national debt has long-term implications, particularly for future generations. International organizations, such as the World Bank and the United Nations, emphasize the importance of sustainable fiscal policies to avoid burdening future generations with excessive debt. They provide guidance and technical support to governments in managing their national debt and promoting fiscal responsibility.

Overspending and increased money supply also have implications beyond national borders. International organizations, such as the World Trade Organization (WTO) and the World Economic Forum (WEF), monitor the impact of US economic policies on global financial markets and international trade. By fostering dialogue and cooperation, they aim to mitigate potential disruptions and maintain stability in the global economy.

The political implications of overspending and increased money supply cannot be ignored. International organizations, such as the International Monetary Fund (IMF) and the World Bank, work with governments to promote transparent and accountable policies. They provide technical assistance and policy recommendations to ensure that political decisions align with long-term economic stability.

In conclusion, international organizations play a crucial role in addressing the global economic challenges arising from the continuous overspending and the printing of more American dollars in the US. Their expertise, guidance, and coordination are essential in mitigating the potential risks and vulnerabilities to the US economy. By collaborating with governments and promoting sustainable economic policies, these organizations contribute to maintaining stability, reducing inequality, and fostering inclusive economic growth.

Chapter 9: The Political Implications of Overspending and Increased Money Supply on Government Policies and Decision-Making

The Political Dynamics of Budgeting and Spending

In today's economic landscape, the issue of budgeting and spending has taken center stage, captivating economists and the public alike. This subchapter delves into the intricate political dynamics that surround the crucial decisions made by governments regarding their fiscal policies. By exploring the impact of overspending and increased money supply on various aspects of the US economy, we gain a deeper understanding of the potential risks and vulnerabilities that could arise due to continuous overspending and printing more American dollars.

One of the foremost concerns is the impact of overspending and increased money supply on inflation rates. As the government pumps more money into the economy, the purchasing power of the dollar diminishes, leading to higher prices for goods and services. This has a direct effect on consumers and businesses, eroding their ability to maintain a stable standard of living.

Foreign debt plays a significant role in exacerbating the US deficit crisis. The accumulation of debt from foreign nations puts the US economy in a vulnerable position, as it becomes increasingly reliant on external funding. This reliance not only affects the deficit but also undermines the nation's sovereignty and economic independence.

The long-term consequences of printing more American dollars on the value of the currency cannot be ignored. As the supply of dollars increases, their value depreciates, leading to a decline in the purchasing power of individuals and businesses. This erosion of value has far-reaching implications for both domestic and international trade.

Overspending also has a direct connection to income inequality in the US. The gap between the rich and the poor widens as government resources are disproportionately allocated, often benefiting the affluent at the expense of the marginalized. This disparity not only hampers social cohesion but also weakens the overall economic fabric of the nation.

Furthermore, the economic implications of overspending and increased money supply on small businesses cannot be understated. These enterprises, often the backbone of the economy, face numerous challenges, including reduced access to credit and increased competition from larger corporations. This stifles innovation, job creation, and economic growth.

The US deficit also has a profound effect on interest rates and borrowing costs. As the government borrows more to finance its overspending, interest rates rise, making it more expensive for businesses and individuals to access credit. This can hinder investment and economic expansion, leading to a slowdown in overall economic activity.

The relationship between overspending, the national debt, and its impact on future generations cannot be ignored. The burden of excessive debt falls on the shoulders of future taxpayers, constraining their economic opportunities and limiting their ability to thrive.

Moreover, overspending and increased money supply have implications beyond domestic borders. The influence of these actions on global financial markets and international trade is significant. Currency devaluation, trade imbalances, and market volatility are just a few of the potential consequences that can disrupt global economic stability.

The political implications of overspending and increased money supply on government policies and decision-making cannot be overlooked. As politicians strive to meet short-term goals and gain popularity, they often prioritize spending over fiscal responsibility. This can lead to a vicious cycle of overspending and jeopardize the long-term economic health of the nation.

In conclusion, the potential risks and vulnerabilities of the US economy due to continuous overspending and printing more American dollars are diverse and multifaceted. From inflation rates and income inequality to small businesses and global financial markets, the impact of these actions is far-reaching. It is imperative that economists and the public alike understand these dynamics to foster informed discussions and advocate for responsible fiscal policies that ensure the stability and prosperity of future generations.

The Influence of Special Interest Groups on Economic Policies

Special interest groups play a significant role in shaping economic policies in the United States. These groups, representing various industries and sectors, exert influence through lobbying, campaign contributions, and other means. Understanding their influence is crucial for economists and the public alike, as it sheds light on the potential risks and vulnerabilities of the US economy due to continuous overspending and printing more American dollars.

One of the key impacts of overspending and increased money supply is inflation rates. Special interest groups often push for policies that benefit their industries, leading to increased government spending. This excess spending, coupled with the injection of more money into the economy, can result in higher inflation rates, eroding the purchasing power of the public and affecting their standard of living.

Foreign debt also exacerbates the US deficit crisis. Special interest groups may advocate for policies that encourage borrowing from foreign nations to finance government spending. However, this reliance on foreign debt puts the US economy at risk, as it increases the vulnerability to external shocks and limits policy autonomy.

Printing more American dollars has long-term consequences on the value of the currency. When the money supply is increased, the value of the currency can decrease, leading to a depreciation. This depreciation can have adverse effects on trade and investment, as it makes imported goods more expensive and reduces the attractiveness of US assets to foreign investors.

Overspending is also connected to income inequality in the US. Special interest groups often lobby for policies that favor their industries, leading to a concentration of wealth in the hands of a few. This exacerbates income inequality, as the gap between the rich and the poor widens, hindering social mobility and economic growth.

Moreover, the implications of overspending and increased money supply on small businesses are significant. These businesses, often lacking the resources and influence of larger corporations, face challenges when government policies favor certain industries. This can stifle competition, hinder innovation, and limit the growth potential of small businesses, which are vital for job creation and economic development.

The US deficit also affects interest rates and borrowing costs. Excessive government spending leads to a higher demand for borrowing, increasing interest rates and making it more expensive for businesses and individuals to borrow money. This can hinder investment and economic growth, as businesses may be reluctant to take on additional debt.

The national debt resulting from overspending has severe implications for future generations. Special interest groups may prioritize short-term gains over long-term sustainability, burdening future generations with the responsibility of repaying the debt. This can limit their opportunities, increase taxation, and hinder economic prosperity.

Furthermore, overspending and increased money supply have implications on global financial markets and international trade. The US economy is interconnected with the global economy, and policies that disrupt this balance can have ripple effects worldwide. This can lead to currency fluctuations, trade imbalances, and financial instability, affecting not only the US but also other nations.

The influence of special interest groups on economic policies also has political implications. Overspending and increased money supply can sway government policies and decision-making, as these groups often have significant lobbying power. This can lead to policies that prioritize the interests of certain industries or sectors, rather than the overall welfare of the economy and its citizens.

In conclusion, special interest groups have a substantial influence on economic policies in the United States, with implications ranging from inflation rates and income inequality to global financial markets and future generations. Understanding the potential risks and vulnerabilities of the US economy due to continuous overspending and printing more American dollars is crucial for economists and the public alike. By recognizing the impact of special interest groups on economic policies, stakeholders can work towards more sustainable and equitable economic practices.

The Role of Public Opinion and Elections in Shaping Government Actions

Public opinion and elections play a vital role in shaping government actions, especially when it comes to addressing the potential risks and vulnerabilities of the US economy due to continuous overspending and printing more American dollars. This subchapter explores the significant influence of public opinion and elections on various aspects of the economy, shedding light on the consequences and implications of government actions.

One of the key areas affected by overspending and increased money supply is inflation rates. Public opinion and elections can influence government policies aimed at controlling inflation. The impact of overspending and increased money supply on inflation rates is a matter of concern for economists and the public alike. By electing representatives who prioritize responsible economic policies, the public can contribute to mitigating the risks associated with rising inflation.

Foreign debt also plays a crucial role in exacerbating the US deficit crisis. Public opinion and elections can shape government actions regarding foreign debt by electing leaders who prioritize reducing and managing this debt. By electing representatives who advocate for responsible fiscal policies and debt reduction strategies, the public can influence the government's approach to tackling the deficit crisis.

The long-term consequences of printing more American dollars on the value of the currency are another concern. Public opinion and elections can influence government actions by electing leaders who prioritize maintaining a stable and strong currency. The value of the currency affects the purchasing power of citizens and impacts international trade. By voting for representatives who prioritize currency stability, the public can safeguard the value of the dollar and protect economic interests.

Overspending also has implications for income inequality and small businesses. The connection between overspending and income inequality in the US can be addressed through public opinion and elections. By electing representatives who prioritize policies that support small businesses and promote economic equality, the public can shape government actions to reduce income disparities and create a more equitable economy.

Furthermore, the US deficit has an impact on interest rates and borrowing costs. Public opinion and elections can shape government actions by electing representatives who prioritize responsible fiscal policies that aim to reduce the deficit. By influencing government decisions on deficit reduction, the public can contribute to maintaining favorable interest rates and affordable borrowing costs.

The national debt and its impact on future generations is another area influenced by public opinion and elections. By electing representatives who prioritize reducing the national debt, the public can shape government actions that safeguard the economic well-being of future generations.

Overspending and increased money supply also have implications for global financial markets and international trade. Public opinion and elections can influence government actions by electing leaders who prioritize responsible economic policies that foster healthy international trade relationships and promote stability in global financial markets.

Lastly, public opinion and elections have political implications on government policies and decision-making regarding overspending and increased money supply. By electing representatives who prioritize responsible fiscal policies, the public can influence government decisions and contribute to sound economic governance.

In conclusion, public opinion and elections play a critical role in shaping government actions in response to the potential risks and vulnerabilities of the US economy due to continuous overspending and printing more American dollars. By actively engaging in the electoral process and voting for representatives who prioritize responsible economic policies, economists and the public can influence government actions and mitigate the potential risks associated with overspending and increased money supply.

Chapter 10: The Potential Risks and Vulnerabilities of the US Economy Due to Continuous Overspending and Printing More American Dollars

The Threat of Hyperinflation and Economic Collapse

In recent years, the United States economy has been plagued by a dangerous trend of overspending and an excessive increase in the money supply. This subchapter will delve into the potential risks and vulnerabilities that this continuous overspending and printing of more American dollars pose to the US economy.

One of the most immediate concerns is the impact on inflation rates. As the government continues to spend beyond its means and pump more money into circulation, the value of the dollar diminishes. This leads to a rise in prices for everyday goods and services, eroding the purchasing power of consumers and causing a decrease in their standard of living. Economists and the public need to be aware of this threat and its implications.

Foreign debt plays a significant role in exacerbating the US deficit crisis. As the government borrows more money from foreign countries, it becomes increasingly dependent on them. This dependency not only weakens the nation's financial independence but also exposes it to potential manipulation by foreign powers. It is crucial for economists and the public to understand the implications of this relationship and its impact on the overall economic stability of the country.

Printing more American dollars may provide short-term relief, but it comes with long-term consequences. This continuous printing of money leads to a devaluation of the currency, making it less attractive to foreign investors. As a result, the value of the dollar declines, affecting not only international trade but also the ability of Americans to maintain a high standard of living. The long-term impact on the value of the currency needs to be carefully considered.

Overspending is not just an economic issue; it also contributes to income inequality within the United States. As the government spends more on programs and subsidies, it often neglects the needs of small businesses. This disparity in resource allocation exacerbates income inequality and hinders the growth of small businesses, which are the backbone of the economy. Economists and the public must recognize the link between overspending and income inequality and advocate for policies that promote a more equitable distribution of resources.

The US deficit also has implications for interest rates and borrowing costs. As the national debt continues to rise, the government must borrow more to finance its obligations. This increased demand for borrowing drives up interest rates, making it more expensive for businesses and individuals to access credit. These higher borrowing costs can have a stifling effect on economic growth and must be carefully managed.

Perhaps the most concerning aspect of continuous overspending and increased money supply is the burden it places on future generations. As the national debt balloons, future generations will inherit the consequences of these actions. The economic stability of the country is at risk, and economists and the public must take action to prevent this burden from falling on the shoulders of future generations.

The influence of overspending extends beyond national borders, impacting global financial markets and international trade. The United States' economic policies have far-reaching consequences, as they affect the stability of global markets and trade relationships. It is essential for economists and the public to recognize the interconnectedness of the global economy and the potential risks associated with US overspending.

Lastly, overspending and increased money supply have significant political implications. Government policies and decision-making are often influenced by the need to address economic challenges caused by overspending. This can result in suboptimal policies that prioritize short-term relief over long-term stability. Understanding these political implications is crucial for economists and the public to effectively advocate for responsible economic practices.

In conclusion, the continuous overspending and printing of more American dollars pose significant threats and vulnerabilities to the US economy. From the impact on inflation rates and income inequality to the long-term consequences on the value of the currency and the burden on future generations, the risks are numerous. Understanding and addressing these potential risks is essential for economists and the public to ensure the stability and prosperity of the US economy.

The Challenges of Managing a Growing National Debt

As the United States continues to face the consequences of continuous overspending and an increased money supply, the challenges of managing a growing national debt are becoming more evident. This subchapter aims to shed light on the potential risks and vulnerabilities that the US economy is facing due to these unsustainable practices. It addresses economists and the public, providing crucial insights into various aspects of this issue.

One of the immediate concerns is the impact of overspending and increased money supply on inflation rates. The excessive injection of money into the economy can lead to a rise in prices, eroding the purchasing power of citizens. This not only affects individuals but also has broader implications for businesses and the overall economy.

Moreover, foreign debt plays a significant role in exacerbating the US deficit crisis. As the national debt continues to grow, the reliance on foreign creditors becomes more pronounced. This reliance puts the US economy at risk, as it becomes vulnerable to changes in global economic conditions and the actions of foreign lenders.

Printing more American dollars to cover the deficit also has long-term consequences on the value of the currency. The continuous increase in the money supply undermines the trust and confidence in the US dollar, potentially leading to a devaluation and loss of purchasing power domestically and internationally.

The connection between overspending and income inequality in the US cannot be overlooked. Excessive government spending often fails to address the root causes of inequality and may exacerbate the wealth gap. This has far-reaching social and political implications and can hinder the overall economic growth of the nation.

Small businesses, the backbone of the US economy, are particularly affected by overspending and increased money supply. The economic implications for these enterprises are wide-ranging, including reduced access to credit, increased costs, and decreased competitiveness, ultimately stifling innovation and job creation.

The US deficit also has a direct impact on interest rates and borrowing costs. As the debt continues to rise, the government needs to borrow more, leading to an increase in interest rates. This not only affects government spending but also impacts the cost of borrowing for businesses and individuals.

The connection between overspending, the national debt, and its impact on future generations is a matter of great concern. The burden of repayment falls on the shoulders of future generations, limiting their opportunities and potentially hindering economic growth and prosperity.

Overspending also has a significant influence on global financial markets and international trade. The US economy's instability can have ripple effects worldwide, causing market volatility and disrupting global economic stability.

Furthermore, overspending and increased money supply have significant political implications. Government policies and decision-making are often influenced by the need to manage the national debt, potentially limiting the ability to address other critical issues.

Ultimately, the continuous overspending and printing of more American dollars pose severe risks and vulnerabilities to the US economy. As this subchapter explores, the consequences range from inflation and income inequality to impacts on small businesses, interest rates, and future generations. The global financial markets and international trade, as well as government policies and decision-making, are also at stake. It is crucial for economists and the public to understand these challenges and work towards sustainable economic practices to secure a stable and prosperous future for the United States.

The Importance of Fiscal Responsibility for Long-Term Economic Stability

In today's complex and interconnected global economy, the concept of fiscal responsibility has become increasingly crucial for long-term economic stability. Overspending and the continuous printing of more American dollars pose significant risks and vulnerabilities to the US economy, impacting various aspects of our society. This subchapter aims to shed light on the importance of fiscal responsibility and its implications for economists and the general public.

One of the primary concerns associated with overspending and increased money supply is its impact on inflation rates. When the government spends more than its revenue, it often resorts to printing more money, leading to an excess supply of currency. This, in turn, can drive up inflation rates, eroding the purchasing power of individuals and businesses. Economists must recognize the detrimental effects of inflation and advocate for responsible fiscal policies to maintain price stability and protect the economy from unnecessary risks.

Furthermore, foreign debt plays a significant role in exacerbating the US deficit crisis. As the government accumulates debt from foreign entities, the burden on future generations increases. The long-term consequences of this trend include higher interest rates, reduced investment, and limited economic growth potential. It is crucial for economists and the public to understand the implications of foreign debt on the overall fiscal health of the nation and work towards reducing reliance on external financing.

Moreover, continuous overspending and the printing of more American dollars can have adverse effects on the value of the currency. As the supply of dollars increases, its value depreciates in relation to other currencies. This can have far-reaching consequences, including reduced purchasing power in international markets and increased costs for imported goods. Economists must highlight the importance of maintaining a stable currency and advocate for responsible fiscal policies to safeguard the value of the American dollar.

Additionally, overspending has been linked to income inequality in the US. When the government allocates a significant portion of its resources to certain sectors or programs, it can exacerbate the wealth gap and hinder economic mobility. Small businesses, in particular, bear the brunt of overspending and increased money supply, as they often struggle to compete with larger corporations that benefit from government support.

It is essential to recognize the economic implications of overspending on small businesses and strive towards a more equitable distribution of resources.

The US deficit also has a direct impact on interest rates and borrowing costs. As the government increases its borrowing to finance its spending, the demand for credit rises, leading to higher interest rates. This, in turn, affects borrowing costs for individuals, businesses, and the government itself. Economists must emphasize the connection between overspending and interest rates to promote responsible fiscal policies that balance public investments without burdening future generations with excessive debt.

Furthermore, the national debt resulting from continuous overspending poses significant risks to future generations. As the debt accumulates, future taxpayers will bear the burden of repayment, limiting their economic opportunities and hampering intergenerational equity. Economists and the public must recognize the long-term consequences of overspending and advocate for sustainable fiscal policies that prioritize the well-being of future generations.

The influence of overspending extends beyond domestic borders, impacting global financial markets and international trade. The US economy plays a crucial role in the global economy, and any destabilization can have widespread implications. Overspending and increased money supply can lead to currency devaluation, affecting trade balances, investment flows, and overall market confidence. It is essential to understand and address these risks to maintain a stable and prosperous global economic system.

Moreover, overspending and increased money supply have political implications, influencing government policies and decision-making. Politicians often face short-term pressures to boost the economy through spending without considering the long-term consequences. Economists must provide informed analysis and recommendations that prioritize fiscal responsibility and advocate for policies that promote sustainable economic growth.

In conclusion, the potential risks and vulnerabilities of the US economy due to continuous overspending and printing more American dollars are significant. Economists and the public must recognize the importance of fiscal responsibility for long-term economic stability. By understanding the impact of overspending on inflation rates, foreign debt, currency value, income inequality, small businesses, interest rates, national debt, global financial markets, international trade, and political decision-making, we can work towards implementing responsible fiscal policies that safeguard the future of our economy and ensure a prosperous nation for generations to come.